The Return of
Big J

by

George Arthur Lareau

SUFI GEORGE BOOKS
PHOENIX

Chapter 1

"What the fuck! Motherfucker! And so on and so forth!" Big J hollered in Aramaic as he looked around at the endless desert landscape. "Where the fuck am I now?" There was no one in sight.

He picked up a handful of the stony ground and watched it slip through his fingers.

He had just appeared at this spot near Quartzsite in a bright flash moments ago.

He looked around more carefully and he saw in the distance what looked like a person. So he headed that way.

It was a saguaro cactus but Big J didn't know that and he kicked it for not answering his questions, and got a spine in his toe.

"Fuck! What armor is this?" he shouted. "Take that suit off and let me kick your ass! What planet is this, for fuck's sake? And so on and so forth!"

After pulling out the spine, Big J looked around again. There was nothing to see, just scattered scrubby bushes.

Then he heard a strange sound, a sound that he had never heard before. In the distance, the source of the sound came into sight. It was an ATV. It was Keefer, coming to check out the flash of light he had seen.

"What the hell is that?" Big J marveled. "It growls without stopping to breathe!"

Big J watched the growing cloud of dust as Keefer approached. The dust was familiar, like from a galloping donkey, but the ATV was no donkey.

Keefer arrived, stared at Big J, shut off his engine, dismounted, and walked up to Big J.

"Dude, you lost out here?" Keefer asked.

"He's a human for sure," Big J thought, "but what the fuck is he saying?

"Maybe I'm still dreaming," he thought, "because shit like this just doesn't exist. But it can't be a dream because this materialization really happened."

He shouted at Keefer, who didn't understand him at all, "I have no fucking idea where I am! Where the fuck am I? Everything is fucking messed up! Can't you speak Aramaic? And so on and so forth!"

So Keefer said, "That's quite an eagle beak you've

got there, dude!" He touched his nose and pointed to Big J's nose.

Big J wondered, "Fuck, am I supposed to pick my nose? What the fuck?"

Keefer wasn't sure what to do. The guy clearly needed help. He wasn't even carrying a bag and his robe had no pockets.

He looked like a hippie with long hair, long beard, and sandals. But what the fuck was he saying? Keefer decided to take him back to camp to see what his friends thought.

It occurred to Keefer that Big J was an alien hippie and the big flash he saw was the space ship. But he couldn't see any evidence of a space ship, so he wasn't sure. Still, alien seemed to be a good guess.

He gestured long enough for Big J to get it, and Big J hopped on the ATV. They rode off in another cloud of dust.

"Well, I have to go fucking somewhere," Big J thought. "I'll just see where he's taking me."

Keefer pulled into the middle of a scattered circle of five RVs. The campers were gathered under the big tree, talking and smoking weed.

"Hey, everybody! Look what I got! A motherfucking alien hippie!" Keefer shouted. "He talks in some fucked up language and I couldn't get anything out of him."

Everybody stood up at once and approached Big J, studying him closely, getting him to speak, murmuring among themselves.

Big J did speak because he had questions and he wanted answers, but no one understood a word of it. And so on and so forth.

Greg got the idea of using the translator app on his phone, and suggested it. They began at the top of the long list of languages.

"Can you understand this language?" they recorded. They all listened to one translation after another until they got to Hebrew when Big J's eyes lit up.

"Hebrew!" they exclaimed.

"And not even halfway through the alphabet!" Joker joked.

"Anybody speak Hebrew?" asked Greg. Nobody answered.

"Well, let's translate some questions into Hebrew," Roland said, and they proceeded to do just that.

"Who are you and where are you from?"

Big J didn't answer, although his wide eyes showed that he understood the translation. He was too mystified by the phone. There was no explanation for its existence. It was even stranger than the ATV.

He replied in Hebrew. Greg didn't get the recorder on in time, and gestured for Big J to repeat it. This time, the translation worked, spitting out English words.

"Nazareth, and so on and so forth."

Big J continued to talk, but the recording was full at this point, so they all listened to the translation. They broke out in a buzz.

"Where the fuck is Nazareth? Illinois?"

"Probably, they got all the Bible name towns there!"

"Well, he didn't walk here from no fucking Illinois!"

"Didn't walk here from no fucking Middle East, either!

"Well, let's ask him again who he is," Greg said.

"Who are you? Are you an alien?"

"No such thing," the translator said.

"I'd take that as a no," Joker said.

"Let's ask how we can help him."

"Food, water," was the response.

"Well, let's all sit the fuck down and feed this dude," Roland said.

"And look," Greg said, " If we're going to depend on the translator app with this guy, let's write down our questions ahead of time."

Keefer picked up the staff he was carving when he'd been sitting there and saw the flash, leaned it against the tree and sat himself down. Everyone sat down except Big J who was still staring at everything in disbelief and confusion.

"Here, have a beer." Keefer tossed a beer to Big J who fumbled the catch.

"Here's some food, called a burrito. Buh ri to," Roland said.

They began their list of questions for the translator. It would be a slow process because half the time the translator didn't get the dictation right and the question had to be typed.

The first question they agreed on was, "Who the fuck are you really?"

Next, "Is your home on this planet?"

Next, suggested by Keefer, "How the fuck did you get here?"

"Do you have a space ship?"

"What the fuck was that flash of light all about?"

"What other languages do you speak?"

And that was enough of a list to occupy them for some hours, including time for discussion of Big

—

J's answers. The translation into English from Hebrew was itself sometimes suspect and that required discussion and sometimes rephrasing of the question.

So, in the same order, here are Big J's answers:

"I am a prophet."

"My home is on this planet."

"Fuck, that rules out the alien theory," Joker complained.

"I got here by materializing."

"So what's that? Like just appearing? Out of nowhere?" Greg asked.

"Sounds like it, " Roland said.

"No such thing as a space ship."

"That's it! He's an just an ignorant asshole!" Joker said.

"The flash of materialization."

"Okay, now we're fucking getting somewhere," Big Don said. "Materialization happens in flashes, everybody got that?"

"Aramaic and Latin."

"Aramaic and fucking Latin!" Keefer said. "A whole lot of fucking good that will do!"

—

"You know what?" Joker shouted, springing up from his chair. "This guy is from the past! He's a time traveler! They always appear in flashes! You've seen that, right? Fuck, that's it! An actual fucking time traveler!"

"And he doesn't speak any languages that people ever heard about, like recently, that is," Big Don said, "so you could be right. Asshole, there aren't any time travelers! Especially from the fucking past!"

Greg summed up the session, saying, "So we have a prophet from the past who speaks ancient languages," Greg said.

"Oh, come off it!" Joker interrupted. "What about the flash? He said it was materialization, so before the flash he wasn't materialized, or his space ship either, and only he materialized and the space ship never did, so I still think he's a fucking alien, a fucking alien! Or a time traveler, maybe."

Big Don said, "We could try passing him off as the fucking second coming. Might be something in it, who the fuck knows?"

"Look, we have to figure out how to communicate with this guy. I'm going to try using the translator app to teach him some English."

Later, all heard Greg shout in exasperation, "Fuck me!"

He had been teaching English with the translator for four hours and so far Big J learned to say the words food and water, and that was all. None of the Q&A translations had taught him anything.

"This isn't working! How the fuck do we teach English to this asshole!"

Roland suggested getting a teacher from a synagogue, but Big Don and Keefer weren't sure they wanted anyone else involved in this mystery yet. Everything about this Hebrew time traveler was totally fucking messed up, and they wanted to figure it out first.

"Fuck it," Big Don said. "He knows how to say food and water, so he'll survive! And he don't need to know how to say shit, just find a bush."

Keefer took the translator and told Big J, "You can bunk and shower with me for now."

And so, Big J was accepted as part of the group and said food and water as needed.

Meanwhile, Big J was listening intently to every word they uttered. He found that it was a strange language, something new, but they repeated a lot of words, like fuck, so he was able to pick up words and meanings.

They had given up on asking him questions with the translator, and now he sat quietly, munching on a burrito, watching the sunset, and listening to the language. The others ignored him for the time being.

Two weeks later, they were all still arguing over who Big J really was. An alien? A prophet? A time traveler? A hippie lost in the desert?

Big J had succeeded in learning their English in those two weeks, and now he began to talk.

"Why the fuck don't you just ask me?" he said. "I'm sitting right here!"

"What the fuck?" Joker said, jumping up. "You fucking son of a bitch! I knew you could speak English, you fucking fake!"

They were stunned to hear him speak so clearly. He talked like one of them. They stared at Big J and they stared at each other.

"Hey! I saw this shit in a movie, The Thirteenth Warrior or some shit like that, the guy learned the language just by listening," Joker said.

"No shit? But that's a movie, asshole!" Big Don said.

"Well, fuck anyway, let's do just ask him, now that he can talk," Greg said.

"So dude, who the fuck are you and where the fuck do you come from?" Greg asked. "Some of us think you're an alien from outer space, and over there they think you're a time traveler from the past. And Big Don doesn't give a fuck who you are, he just wants to make some money off of you."

Big J laughed. It was his first laugh in the two weeks he had been camped here. "You can call me by my cool dude name, Big J, and I come from up there or out there somewhere, I'm not clear on that."

"Come on, don't fuck around," Greg said. "Before you said you were from Nazareth. What was that the fuck about?"

"Well, that was a while back. Nazareth was a long time ago," Big J answered. "A long fucking time ago. I hardly remember it. But I remember almost nothing about other places, so I said Nazareth."

"Okay, so tell us how we found you alone in the middle of the desert. Where did you come from that day? You said you materialized. Materialized from what, from where?" Greg went on.

"Well, that's the thing," Big J said. "Everything is always materializing, so that wasn't anything special."

"What the fuck are you, a fucking quantum physicist now? I want to know where you lived before you showed up here."

"That would be villages."

"What about the prophet business you said. What the fuck is that about?" Roland asked.

Big J shrugged his shoulders and said, "Oh, that was nothing, really. I had this vivid dream one night and told my friends about it and they are thinking, like, I'm talking about some other reality, and they started calling me a fucking prophet.

"This was back in Nazareth. It spread a little from there, but it never amounted to anything. They soon went their different ways and that was that. There were lots of prophets then. Then the fucking government sons of bitches killed me and that was the end of this prophet."

"Okay, so now you're killed, what came next?" Greg asked.

"Oh, I got born a few more times. Nothing remarkable in those lives, though. And then floating around but not here, lots of fucking floating around."

"Are you a prophet?"

"You know, my lives after that were shit. I just wanted to go around a few more times to see if my prophet business was growing, but in fact there wasn't shit happening with that. A failed venture.

"That prophet episode was my highlight, a lifetime where some people thought I was important. So prophet comes to mind when I want to describe myself. But I really don't remember much about it. I mean, fuck, dude, that was like two thousand fucking years ago!"

"So what are you doing here now?" Greg asked.

"Well, you know, events are created by thoughts and it seems that enough people have been expecting me to return that it created the energy that brought me here."

"To the middle of the desert?" Greg chuckled.

"Yeah, that was fucked up. I guess there were too many signals being sent out, you know, from too many different directions, and here I am at the average location."

"Who do you suppose these people are, the ones who are sending you the signals to return?"

"I don't know, I just feel the energy."

"How many, do you suppose?"

"Oh, I don't know, enough to make me materialize. Why?"

"Look, Big J," Big Don interrupted. "I don't know where the fuck you've been hiding for two thousand years, but I got to tell you, you are in one big fucking mess. If I believe you. Maybe I believe you. But this prophet business is about to bite you in the ass big time."

"What are you talking about?"

"Okay, for starters, do you know about Constantine? He was a Roman emperor."

"That must have been after my time."

"Anyway, he turned the story about you, a half-ass prophet, into the world's biggest sensation. There probably isn't a person in the world who doesn't know you by the name Jesus Christ."

"Jesus? Dude, that was my name! In the prophet

days. But what's the Christ part?"

"That got tacked on to show that you are secretly God."

"Well, fuck me!"

"Yeah, huh?"

The others had been listening intently, not interrupting. Then the talking stopped and everyone stared expectantly at Big J.

Big Don burst out, "Well damn it, are you the fucking second fucking coming or fucking not, damn it! Easy fucking question!"

"Like I fucking even know what that is," Big J said.

"Look, Big Don," Greg explained. "He probably really is the second coming but it doesn't amount to shit. It's not what people were expecting, all razzle-dazzle like. This is Jesus, a prophet from Nazareth who never amounted to shit.

"So if you want to cash in on the second coming, you're starting pretty much from scratch with a homeless hippie."

"What. The. Fuck," Big Don said in dismay.

Chapter 2

"Can you do that flash thing again?" Big Don wasn't giving up on finding a way to cash in on Big J's second coming.

"Nope. The flash brought me here and I'm still here, so how can I do it again?" Big J shrugged.

"Well, maybe we can use laser lights," Big Don grumbled. "Anybody got laser lights?"

"Maybe we can get that space ship to materialize. That would be fucking spectacular!" Joker said, waving his arms.

"There's no fucking space ship in the second coming scenario, asshole!" Big Don screamed. "Will you just forget about the fucking space ship? We're going with the prophet. No fucking space ships!

"So, look, Big J, let's talk about this. When you were a prophet before, you probably just walked around and sat on rocks, right?" Big Don asked.

"Well, duh, I told you I was pretty fucking small-time." Big J said.

"And you've been out of touch, shall we say, with what goes on in the world, right?"

"Oh, I don't know. I can see that camping in the desert with wheelhouses is new."

"Call them fucking RVs, dude. Anyway, what I want to talk about is that a lot has changed in the world and we need to get you prepared.

"So how about helping out here, assholes. Let's prepare Big J for his debut in the modern world," Big Don went on. "Mainly, what fucking assholes most people are. And you got to know how to deal with them."

"Look, Big Don," Big J said, "I've already failed once in the prophet business. Why the fuck would I want to try that again? Couldn't I just get a job? You will recall, propheting got me fucking killed once."

"Yeah, well, I'm sure that was a bitch, but I think you'll be welcomed with open arms today," Big Don said. "You just don't realize the groundwork that has been laid down for the second coming. It's fucking immense! Worldwide!"

Greg spoke up. "And just how the hell are you ever going go persuade anyone, anybody at all, that Big J here is the second coming? You'll need some kind of proof, you know. Even if he isn't.

Maybe especially if he isn't the second coming."

"I can tell about the flash I saw!" Joker waved.

"Like anybody ever believes what you say," Greg said.

"Hold on here, before you go planning my life. You're overlooking one thing. Who the fuck are you guys? I don't really give a shit because you're the only people I know, but the point is I don't know you. You sit around and plan my life without ever filling me in on who the fuck you are!"

"You are certainly right about that," Greg said apologetically. "We have assumed a lot and we are sorry."

"Hi, Big J! Let me introduce myself. I'm Big Don and I'm a wheeler-dealer."

"Hi, Big J! I'm Joker, and nobody ever believes me."

"Hi, Big J! I'm Roland and I make music."

"Hi, Big J! I'm Keefer and I carve sticks."

"Hi, Big J! I'm Greg and I think about shit."

Big J looked around at them and smiled. "Well, what are you doing here? Is this how people live now or what?"

Greg started. "Big J, I suppose we each have our own reasons for being here, but we share the fact that life with the people out there sucks so bad that we walked away from it."

Big Don added, "We just got fucking tired of the dickhead idiots and avaricious bitches."

And Roland, "Two months ago we didn't know each other and now we're like this fucked up family."

Joker piped up. "Hey, Big J! Isn't the second coming supposed to do that cool shit, you know, do a fucking wipeout with an Armageddon or whatever, or whatever shit you got, right? Save the world, man!"

"Now, what in the motherfucking fuck would I know about that? And if second comings include shit agendas like that, there is no way, dude. You want to save the world, go ahead, but do it without me!"

Big Don said, "Hey, we don't got to get into any of that shit! Remember KISS, Keep It Simple, Stupid. We can charge for healings. Not charge, you know, donations. You can do healings, can't you, Big J?"

"Healings? That's the business you have in mind for me?"

"Dude! That's what you're famous for! You're a healer!"

"Well, fuck me," Big J muttered. "I don't remember shit about that. You think I can do it?"

"You tell me. If you can't do it, we'll just fucking fake it like all the other healers out there."

"Well, wait a minute. I do remember this one time I had someone hold a bowl of warm milk in front of this woman's mouth and a tapeworm came out and I smashed its head between two stones and pulled it out."

"Okay, tricks like that are okay, we can do warm milk. But what do you think, can you really heal for real?" Big Don urged.

"Fuck if I know. Any of you dudes got something wrong? We can do a test," Big J suggested.

They looked around at each other. No one seemed to have a complaint. Then Joker said, "Hey, I'm getting a bald spot, look, right here, see it? Can you fix that?"

"Get a fucking wig," Big J answered. "So, any ideas? How I can test my healing powers? It would be fucking cool if I can really do that."

"We can catch a rabbit, injure it, and then you can heal it," Joker said.

"You're going to injure a rabbit," Keefer said. "Really."

"Fuck it all, we don't need a test. I'm not going to do it," Big J said.

"Why the fuck not?" Big Don challenged. "You sit in a chair and you heal. Is that so fucking difficult? Come on, you'd need a driver's license

---

to get any other job."

"So you're giving me a job here," Big J said. "Do you fucking think in your messed up mind that I came here to apply for a fucking job?"

"You can't live off of our burritos forever, Big J," Big Don said. "You got to have some kind of gig that makes money. Healing is the perfect racket for you. For us, really, because we can all make a buck off of this."

"Me, a healer." He paused and kicked the dirt. "Well, who knows, if I could do it before and now here I am, all me again, maybe I can still do it. Who knows?

"Tell you what, if I can do it and it's easy to do, you know, like I don't want any passing out shit, then okay, I'll give it a try. And if I can't heal, than as you say, we'll fucking fake it."

"Now we're talking!" Big Don said, clapping his hands. "Pass me that fucking joint. I got to think now." He sat back, took a long toke, checked out the sky for pretty clouds, and let his mind begin to grind away, constructing his grand plan.

He finished off the joint and reached into his cutoffs for his tin of weed and papers, and rolled another.

They all wore cutoffs except that Greg's shorts had a sewn hem.

"Dudes, I need some cutoffs so I can have pockets like you. This robe ain't for shit for carrying things," Big J pointed out.

Roland said, "I've got a pair that will fit you, let me get them," and he walked to his RV and came back with a pair of cutoffs that he handed to Big J.

Big J slipped them on under his robe and removed the robe.

"Dude! Look at you! Looking all normal and shit!" Joker said. They all showed approval of Big J's new look.

Keefer handed Big J a small carving of a wizard and said, "Here's a little something to put in your pocket."

"Did you carve this, dude? Shit man, you are fucking good!"

Big Don was building his plan with hums and mumbles, getting a vision of it, smiling, and then announcing it. "Yeah, we'll need a revival tent. Set it up right over there. And a security fence so they don't get in without paying, er, donating.

"We'll need a big sign for the suggested donations, strongly suggested donations. Like $50 for a healing, $20 to ask a question, which must be in writing, and $10 for admission.

Joker stood up. "And a concession! Holy this and blessed that shit! And a photo booth, take your picture with Big J!"

"Sounds more like a vision than a plan, Big Don," Greg said.

"Everything starts with the vision, dude!" Big Don retorted.

"You're getting a little carried away, aren't you?" Greg said. "I mean, why the fuck would people want to pay money to see Big J? You need a hook, a pretty good one, and you don't got one."

"Yeah, if you could make the healer gig work for real, that would be a good hook right there," Roland said.

"Considering fucking medical costs these days, fifty bucks would be cheap," Joker said.

"Maybe we really do need to injure a rabbit here," Big Don said slowly. "We need to test this shit out."

"Big J, do you think you can heal a rabbit that has a bullet hole in it?" Keefer asked.

"That depends on what a bullet is," Big J hesitated.

"Damn, you don't know shit, do you?" Big Don exclaimed. "We got to teach you about guns?"

Keefer said, "Come on, I'll show you my rifle. In fact, let's go rabbit hunting." They got the gun, got on his ATV and rode off in a trail of dust.

Then Greg said, "Big Don, you do realize, don't you, that you just fucking appropriated Keefer's discovery?"

"I don't hear him complaining. Besides, he can't

handle this by himself. No way ass-sitting and carving sticks is talent enough. He needs me, needs all of us. "

"Yeah, that may be true, but you just fucking grabbed when you could have been a bit more gracious."

"Yeah, well, who gives a fuck now? I just hope to hell that they come back with a healed rabbit, you know? Because I have no fucking idea how to fake a healing."

"Yeah, it all depends on that. Of course, that would mean that Big J is the real thing, and that could get out of control, Big Don. And if he really can heal, does he need any of us, really?"

"Fuck that. He's a disoriented, ignorant alien. He doesn't even have an ID so that makes him some kind of illegal immigrant. He couldn't even get to town on his own!"

"Well, I can't argue with that. But we need to know if he can heal, because if he can't, I think we've had some interesting conversations and that's about it."

Time passed, joints were passed, burritos were consumed, and then Keefer and Big J returned.

"Where's the fucking rabbit?" Big Don shouted. Keefer held the rabbit in the air.

"Looks fucking dead to me, dude!"

"Well, it is dead, asshole. One shot."

"What about the fucking healing, dude?"

"Figured you would like to watch. Got a problem with that?"

"Fuck, no! Didn't think of that! So Big J, are you ready to give it a shot?"

"I'm not quite sure," Big J said. This rabbit died, it's dead, and that isn't a healing situation. It's more like fucking raising from the dead. So I don't know."

"Well, damn, dude, give it a fucking try!"

So Big J took the rabbit from Keefer, holding it by its long ears. Its eyes were closed. Big J held its face close to his, opened his mouth wide, and exhaled a long, slow breath. And the rabbit wiggled.

"Ya fucking hoo!!" Joker shouted. "It works! It just takes bad breath, fucking amazing! We can bag his breath in balloons and sell it!"

"No way!" Greg exclaimed. "You can really fucking do it? You can really fucking heal? Will it work on people?"

Roland said, "That is totally fucking cool, dude!"

Big J waved the rabbit back and forth. "So what do I do with this fucking rabbit?"

Joker jumped up and headed for the rabbit. "Is the bullet hole still there? Keefer, where did you hit this motherfucker?"

"Damned if I know," Keefer said. I was lucky to hit it at all. It was quite a ways away."

Joker began examining the rabbit for a bullet hole. He couldn't find one. "Not even a scar!" he screamed in frustration. "Nice fucking exhibit without a scar!"

"Well, we can at least tell the fucking story. I say we keep the rabbit," Big Don said.

"When you say keep, who do you mean exactly? I don't want rabbit shit in my RV, so it's not me," Greg said.

"Oh, fuck it, I've got a cage in my trailer," Keefer said. "Does that mean I have to fucking go dig it out?"

"Um, I don't know exactly how long I can stand here holding this rabbit," Big J said.

"I'll give you a hand," Roland said to Keefer. "Meanwhile, let's find a bag or something to put the rabbit in. Give Big J a break, now that he's a real healer."

So they bagged the rabbit, and Keefer and Roland went off to Keefer's trailer and began hunting through the mess of things Keefer sold at flea markets.

"Do rabbits eat burritos?" Joker asked.

"There's no burritos in the desert," Greg said, "so you answered your own question."

"I mean, we have to feed it, right? What do they eat? There's nothing out there in the desert. Maybe they don't have to eat at all, who knows? Besides, we got burritos and we're in the desert, ha ha ha."

"The miracle desert rabbit!" Big Don said. "People will pay to pet it, or feed it. Greg, why don't you google what rabbits eat?"

After a moment, Greg said, "I lost my connection. Just feed it some leaves and see what it likes, fuck."

"Okay, sounds like a plan," Big Don said.

Keefer and Roland returned with the cage, and Big J put the rabbit in, and shook his tired hand.

"So what's our next step now," Big Don said. "We've got to let some motherfuckers know about what we've got here or we'll never make a fucking dime!"

"Let's make a parade in Quartzsite!" Joker said. "We can carry signs and blow our horns! New faith healer here, folks!"

"How about a few of us go into Quartzsite and start a few rumors," Greg suggested. "You know, like tell the rabbit story confidentially to someone. Keefer and Joker go, they can corroborate each other."

"Hey, that's good!" Big Don said. "Great! Now, what about the revival tent and the fence, what can we do about that? We got to get that shit

—

together before we start spreading the word."

"Like any of us are going to pay for that shit," Greg said.

"Oh, fuck it!" Keefer said. "We can just set up a booth and then we can figure out some kind of little gate. We could use my flea market booth, hang the walls on it."

"Fuck, yeah!" Big Don said. "They'll only be coming one at a time anyway!"

"Oh, fuck it. Does that mean I have to fucking go dig it out?" Keefer said.

"I'll give you a hand," Roland said to Keefer.

After a sweaty while, Keefer and Roland had the booth set up. It was covered with canvas on top and on three sides. They chose a site where their camp was out of sight.

"We'll get Greg to get the GPS coordinates for this," Keefer said.

"You think everybody who wants to come here has a GPS?" Roland asked.

"Well, if they can't afford a GPS, then they probably can't make much of a fucking donation, right? So fuck them."

They returned to the camp. "Okay," Keefer announced, "the throne of heaven has been erected."

"Yeah!" Big Don shouted. "You look like you're both ready for a fucking beer!"

"Does it really have a throne?" Joker asked. "Is there a fucking throne in it?"

"Where were we going to find a motherfucking throne in the motherfucking desert, asshole?" Keefer retorted. Then, to Big Don, "Yeah, toss a couple of those beers over here."

"We could probably just use ropes and posts to make a line for people to wait behind," Greg commented. "No way we can fucking afford fencing."

"Okay," Big Don said. "We can do it that way until the money starts rolling in, then we can rent a fucking mobile stage! Okay, who's got some fucking posts and rope?"

Keefer lifted his beer and drank while the others were silent, posts and ropes wise.

"Oh, fuck it! I've got posts and ropes in the trailer. Does that mean I have to fucking go dig them out?" Keefer said.

"I'll give you a hand," Roland said to Keefer.

Chapter 3

Keefer and Joker rode the ATV into Quartzsite. It was off-season for the famous flea market, but there were grizzly vendors who stayed year-round, and they dotted the street with their vans and campers and stalls.

There was no business to be had this time of year, so the vendors congregated to smoke weed and pass the time. Keefer and Joker approached this group, which was in Naked Man's stall.

They knew most of the vendors by name, and when they came close, Keefer shouted, "Hey, Naked Man! Got ass?"

"Got ass? Really?" Joker asked. "What the fuck is that, got ass."

"Okay, fuckhead, your turn. Go ahead," Keefer said.

Joker thought for a moment, and then shouted,

"Hey, Naked Man! Got diseases?"

"Got diseases? Really?" Keefer mocked. Then they were with the group.

"Keefer, Joker, what's up, dudes?" Naked Man greeted.

"Fuck, it's hotter in this tent than it is outside!" Joker bitched. "Why are you in here, anyway?"

"Smoking weed, asshole," Martin said in a low voice.

"Oh, well fuck, I'm already stoned so I'm getting the fuck out of this oven." He stepped outside. After a few moments, they all joined him.

Some of them found things to sit on, but not Naked Man. He was always standing, tall and lanky.

"So how's life at the campsite, you anarchist dudes?" Martin asked.

Joker answered, "Oh, just space aliens with invisible space ships, but it was my mistake."

"Dude, you can fuck up anything! Let me answer!" Keefer said. Then to the others, "Look, I don't want this to go outside of this group, you guys and us in the camp. You got to swear to that or I ain't telling you fucking shit. What do you say?"

"Maybe you ain't got shit to say, dude, you think of that?" Angelo said.

"Ha ha. I'm serious. What do you say?" No one answered. "Believe me, this is worth it. But you can't let it get out. So?"

"What the fuck," Angelo said, "I pledge allegiance to the group. Like anything else is happening." Then the others all agreed.

"Okay, let me tell you this, and this is all true. I shot a rabbit, dead, and this dude who appeared in a flash breathed on it and it came alive again." Keefer began.

"So it was fucking dead, huh? You sure it wasn't just faking because those little motherfuckers will do that!" Angelo said.

Joker felt it was to chime in. "But I saw it! I examined that rabbit for a bullet hole and just couldn't find one. Well, that was after the breathing thing."

"Fuck, dude, you are so out of sequence!" Keefer said in exasperation. "Just wait for me to flip your switch, okay?

"I've killed rabbits before, Angelo. I know a dead animal when I have it in my hands. And it stayed dead throughout the ride back to camp, and it stayed dead while we talked about it. And then Big J breathed on it and it came alive."

Martin asked, "So what is this breathing thing about? And who the fuck is Big J?"

"Big J," Keefer said, "is this healer guy we found in the desert. And like I just fucking told you, he brought this rabbit I shot back to life by breathing on it."

Martin summarized. "And to prove this story, all you have a live rabbit in a cage, a fucking live rabbit in a fucking cage. Dude, you are fucked up, you know that? Some bullshit!"

Joker looked at Keefer and said, "You know what? You know what? You could just fucking shoot the rabbit again!"

"You are a sick motherfucker! But actually, for once you might be right."

Keefer turned to Martin. "Look, maybe this might work, I don't know. This is all new shit to us. But suppose Big J agreed and I shot the rabbit and you're there to make fucking certain that the rabbit is dead, and then Big J does his breathing thing and the rabbit comes alive, if that happens, it wouldn't be bullshit then, would it?"

Martin looked up at Keefer, staring at him, shielding his eyes with his hand. "Do you seriously mean that there is a single chance in hell that that could actually fucking happen?"

"We saw it happen once!" Joker said. "Actually, that took two of us, one to see the rabbit die in the desert and one to see it come alive in camp although both of us saw that, so between us we saw it all."

Naked Man chimed in, "You actually saw a dead rabbit brought back to life. By a healer guy you found in the desert. Okay, let's go with that, what the fuck."

"Like I said, I don't know if Big J will do it..." Keefer said.

"He didn't sweat doing it once, dude!" Joker interrupted.

Keefer continued, "Yeah, it wasn't any big deal to him, so he'll probably be willing to do it again. Just to prove it to you assholes."

"Well then, that is some shit I'd like to fucking see," Martin said.

"Fuck yeah, me too!" Angelo said. The other three vendors nodded their agreement.

"It'll be fifty bucks," Keefer said, "ten bucks apiece if you all come at one time. And if the shit doesn't happen, I'll refund five bucks apiece. No, just fucking with you, I'll give your money back."

"So when do we do this?" Angelo asked.

"We got to check this out with Big J. Then we'll let you know. Meanwhile, get your ten bucks apiece lined up. And no bartering."

Keefer and Joker went back to the camp and gave a full account of their little adventure.

"So do they believe that we can kill the rabbit again and Big J will revive it again?" Greg asked.

"Fuck, I don't know if they believe it or if they're just bored. Either way, they're willing to cough

———

up fifty bucks between them to find out. I told them if it didn't work, I'd refund them," Keefer answered.

"Well, do we believe it?" Greg asked. "What do you think, Big J, can you do it again?"

"Fuck if I know. I didn't know how to do it the first time. But it did work the first time, so maybe I can do it again."

"Well, let's do a test!" Joker jumped up. "Let's shoot the little fucker again and see if Big J can do his thing again!"

"And then?" Roland asked. "Are we just going to keep on shooting this rabbit again and again?"

"Yeah, it'll be amazing! Step right up, folks! See the resurrecting rabbit! Fucking sensational!"

"That is just a little bit fucking sick!" Big Don said. "Now, the test idea is not bad but it's not necessary because our fifty dollar demonstration is a test. So let's not get too fucking gory about this."

"Good idea," Roland said.

"Okay," Big Don settled, "you two go back and tell them that Big J is cool with it and to come on the fuck over."

"Oh," Keefer asked Greg, "did you get the GPS coordinates?"

"Oh, right, here, I wrote them down." Keefer

simply took the paper without saying anything and Greg said, sarcastically, "You're welcome."

He left for Quartzsite again.

Meanwhile, Big Don was getting antsy. He wanted to be sure that they were going to collect that fifty bucks.

"Fuck it, let's do the test! Let's fucking find out if this is going to really fucking work!"

"Well, why the fuck not? I'd like to know," Greg said.

"Let me shoot it this time," Big Don said. He took the rabbit out of the cage and put it on the ground in the middle of the circle they had all stood up to form. He reached into his pocket and took out a small .38 revolver. He walked up to the rabbit."

"Bye, rabbit, see you again soon, we hope."

He aimed at the rabbit's head and fired. The shot demolished its target.

"Fuck, man!" Joker shouted. "You blew its motherfucking head off! There's nothing left for Big J to breathe on! We're fucked!"

They stood around in silence, watching the rabbit remnants drip blood. Finally, Big J said, "What the fuck, I'll give it a try anyway." He picked up the dead rabbit remnants, breathed, and wonder of wonders, it reformed and revived!

"Holy son of a fucking bitch!" Big Don shouted.

"You can really do it, Big J! Shit, dude, you could probably revive, fuck, I don't know, anything!"

Big J said, "I got to tell you, I am personally impressed. This is some hot shit!"

"You are going to be so fucking rich and famous, dude!" Joker said. "I can just see your fucking hundred foot RV!"

"You need an outfit, dude!" Big Don said. "Something like that rag you showed up in, only nice!"

Joker said, "A robe that lights up! Glows in the dark!"

"Oh, get fucking bent, will you," Big Don said.

"What's wrong with the way I look now?" Big J asked. "I look just like you dudes."

"That's the problem," Big Don said. "You're the star of this show and you need to look the part. Look, can you just materialize a clean robe for yourself?"

"I can't do that shit!" Big J said. "I'm fucking lucky I know how to heal, let alone materialize shit."

"You could at least wash your hair and trim your beard," Greg suggested. "You'd stand out then."

Keefer returned and said the five vendors were on their way.

"We did the test!" Joker blurted out. "Big Don blew the rabbit's fucking head off and Big J fixed it right up!"

"What?" Keefer said skeptically. "You mean this shit really actually works? Big J can do it? Again and again with the same rabbit? Well, fuck me!"

"That's fifty bucks a bullet," Big Don said, chuckling. "I'd say we're in business, wouldn't you? Fuck yeah!"

"Hold on!" Big J interrupted. "How long do you think I'm going to keep doing this? Reviving a rabbit isn't much of a fucking life purpose for me."

"Hey, when you get to healing people, that's when it'll get interesting, fucking interesting," Big Don said. "The rabbit is just for starters, an introduction like."

Then, the cloud of dust from the five vendors became visible, so Joker said, "Well, let's go to the site and do our fucking show!"

Big Don grabbed the rabbit cage and headed for his mud truck. Roland and Big J tagged along for the ride. Keefer and Joker got on the ATV. And Greg just sat there. "You can give me the full story when you get back," he said.

The site now boasted a simple canvas booth and a rope fence. Big Don carried a chair from his truck and planted it near the rope entrance, waiting to collect the money.

The others gathered under the booth and soon the vendors arrived. They greeted Big Don who held his hand out for the money. They each gave him ten dollars and Big Don followed them to the booth. Tall, lanky Naked Man's head brushed the top canvas.

"Let's not blow the poor fucker's head off this time," Roland said. "Anybody got a .22?"

They all looked at each other. No one had a small caliber gun. So Big Don said, "Well, I guess we blow the poor motherfucker's head off again."

"Now, nobody disputes that the rabbit is alive, right?" Don said. They crowded around the rabbit cage, watching it be alive.

"This rabbit has been dead twice but it is totally fucking alive now, right? It's not a wind-up rabbit, right?"

They all agreed that the rabbit was indeed fully alive.

"So now I'm going to shoot it," Big Don said, and started to point his gun at the cage.

"Hold it!" Roland said. "Don't shoot through the fucking cage, dude, the bullet might ricochet!"

"I'll hold it up," Keefer said, and he reached into the cage, grabbed the rabbit by the ears and held it up at arm's length. "Let's move away from here to do this," he said. "We don't need this to look like a fucking murder scene."

They walked together a little ways, stopped, Keefer held up the rabbit by the ears, Big Don approached it, pointed the gun at its head and fired.

The carcass of the rabbit fell to the ground, leaving Keefer holding the dripping ears in midair.

"Holy motherfuck!" Angelo shouted. "You blew its motherfucking head off!"

Keefer picked up the carcass and said, "Okay, let's get this little fucker revived." He held the ears in position and held the rabbit in front of Big J.

He challenged the vendors, "This is the same dead rabbit, right? What's left of it? Okay, now watch."

They stood expectantly on tiptoes, crowded around Big J, eyes on the rabbit. Big J took a breath and slowly released it on the rabbit's goulash. It reformed and revived once again.

The vendors all gasped. "No fucking way!" they shouted. "How did you do that?" "Mother-fuck!" "Ho-ly shit!"

The vendors broke into animated conversation, all speaking at once, all on different tracks, and none listening to anyone else; and adding to it, the camp dudes were also talking to everyone, answering questions with answers as nonsensical as the questions.

Big Don quieted things down. "Listen up! Okay, you've seen it and you're the only ones because from now on the rabbit is just our pet. We're not going to shoot it any more. We just wanted some witnesses to back up the story, got it?"

"Well," Martin said, "I witnessed it but I still don't believe it. I mean, what the fucking fuck! Who the fuck is this guy?"

Angelo said, "Yeah, Big J, how about telling us who you are? Where you from, dude? Where did you learn how to do that?"

"Dudes, dudes, slow the fuck down!" Big J said. "I don't even have answers for most of that. I remember being a small-time prophet in Nazareth and getting killed for my trouble.

"I really don't get it at all, but all this time I've been sort of floating around and then there's this build-up of energy coming at me from all directions pulling me back. So don't look at me, dude, I didn't do it. It just happened to me."

"And the healing thing?"

"Beats me," Big J said. "The prophet had that and I guess it transfers to the me that I am now. Don't ask me how the prophet got it."

"And that's your story, then," Angelo said. "Energy pulls you back, you can still heal, and you're 2000 years behind in your education."

Martin said, "So like you're like the second coming, only you're ignorant, homeless, and you have bad breath. Is that about it?" Big J shrugged and nodded.

More animated discussion ensued, and they developed an agreement that it was possible that Big J was indeed the second coming, however poor an excuse he made of it.

"Well, I got to tell you, you are going to be a big surprise to anybody who believes that you are the second coming. In fact, a gigantic disappointment. You're not at all what they're expecting," Angelo said.

Roland said, "The main thing you have to catch up on is Christianity, especially the fundamentalists, because they are fucking all over you."

"There's a religion based on that puny prophet? How in the fuck did that ever happen?" Big J burst out.

"Never mind how," Roland continued. "The point is, they are expecting you to return in a cloud of angels and pull 144,000 of them up into the air with you."

"What?? You're not just fucking with me here? That has got to be the most fucked up ridiculous idea ever! I mean, whatever the fuck for? It's fucking cold up there and then what? Drop like icicles?

"Are people absolutely motherfucking crazy? Does anybody seriously think I could do that? How the fuck would anybody do that?

"And considering I got killed last time," Big J decided, "I'm going to just forget about all that other shit and just be a healer. Might be safer, not to mention possible."

The vendors settled down in a state of information overload.

"So have you considered what you can do with this, Big J?" Martin asked. "I mean, you are on the edge of being rich and famous, dude! Fifty bucks is shit money, you can get thousands at a time for healings!"

"How come everything is about fucking money?" Big J asked. "Healing people is probably a good thing with or without money involved. And all you motherfuckers talk about is money!"

Yeah, well," Big Don began, "money makes the world go around, the world go around, the world go around," singing from Cabaret. "Anyway, I'm getting fucking hungry here. I'm going back to camp and heat up some fucking burritos."

"Yeah, let's go back," Roland said.

"We'll follow you!" Martin said.

"You walk if you do!" Big Don said. "We set up shop out here to keep the dust away from camp!"

"Well, how about we pile into just one vehicle?"

"Oh, fuck, come on."

When they all were gathered back at camp, Big

Don started heating up burritos in his RV's microwave. He brought out enough for the campers and Angelo asked, "Hey, you got more of those? Those smell good!"

"You bet," Big Don said. "Two bucks apiece."

"Well, fucker, okay."

"Me, too," the other vendors said, and that was another ten bucks for Big Don. They wanted to talk but they were mostly all talked out, and just ate quietly.

They had witnessed a miracle. They all saw it. And it blew their minds. There was no way to assess it, to understand it.

Angelo finally said, "Fuck it, I can't get my fucking head around this. Let's go back and get fucking stoned."

The vendors slowly stood up and headed for their one vehicle. They had to drive back to the site to pick up the other two, and then back to Quartzsite, and they were grumbling about that.

Chapter 4

The sun had barely risen when the campers were awakened by distant car horns.

Big Don sat up in bed. "Fuck me! This business starts early!" He went to the front of his RV and blew his horn a few times to awaken the others.

They gathered near the tree, bitching about getting up so early. They all heard the continuous horns and they knew what was up.

"Big J! Can you heal this early?" Greg asked.

"We'll see. But first, anybody got some fucking coffee?" Big J suggested.

"I could use some breakfast," Keefer said. "We don't have to fucking rush over there, do we?"

"You think they'll wear down their batteries, blowing their fucking horns like that?" Joker said.

"You mean, then they'll be stuck in the desert?"

Greg asked.

So they decided to endure the horn blowing and make some coffee and heat up some burritos.

"Okay," Big Don said between mouthfuls, "when we get there, you go in the booth, Big J, and I'll sit at the rope entrance, and you three organize those people into a single file.

"Here's what I'm thinking. They can get a healing for fifty bucks, a question answered for fifty bucks and it has to be in writing, and ten bucks just to sit and listen. Sound okay with everybody?"

"Fuck the questions, Big Don," Big J said. "I'm just doing healings."

"Okay, okay, ten bucks to watch fifty buck healings. So you three explain this to those assholes, and if they don't have the cash, tell them to go to the rear of the line. They still won't get in, but they won't know that, and so they won't make trouble while waiting."

It was a chilly morning, and chugging the hot coffee felt good.

"Before we go, let's make some signs to post out there, like we're open from ten to two, and blowing your horn three times is fucking enough," Roland proposed.

"Good idea," Greg said. "Who's got some stuff to make a fucking sign with?"

Nobody spoke. Finally, Keefer said, "Fuck me! Am I the only one who has anything? What the fuck have you dudes got in your fucking RVs, anyway?"

Roland said, "I'll give you a hand.

The sign read:

> Open 10am to 2pm
> At 9:45am, blow your horn three times.
> Watching $10
> Healing $50
> Donations subject to change.

Keefer led the way with his ATV, Big J in tow. Big Don drove the other three in his mud truck. When they arrived, they saw five vehicles and about fourteen people milling around. They set up the table at the rope entrance and taped the sign along the front of the table. The milling turned into sign reading, and one man said, "Fifty bucks? We were told ten bucks! What the fuck!"

Big Don said, "We haven't told anybody ten bucks so I don't know where you got that. Besides, ten bucks is for rabbits. So are you here for a healing or what?"

"Well, what the fuck do I get for ten bucks, then?" the man asked.

"You get to watch other people getting healed. It'll be amazing shit."

Twelve of the fourteen arrivals paid the ten bucks and took a squat in front of the booth. The other two were like just roadies.

It was then that Big Don realized that everyone was there to watch healings, but none of them was there to get healed and so what the fuck was there for them to watch?

"Fuck!" he shouted in frustration. "What the fuck do we do now?"

"Hey, let's break somebody's arm! Or Leg!" Joker said.

"How does that make us fifty bucks, asshole!" Big Don said. "I guess we wait until two o'clock and see if anybody shows up that wants some fucking motherfucking healing!"

They gathered in the shade of the booth. They looked at the people squatted in front of the booth, in the sun.

"It is a little cooler in here," Greg said. "We can stand here and watch those poor bastards sweat."

"Fuck, dudes!" Roland said. "We can't just let them fucking sit in the sun for four hours!"

"So you want to invite them in the booth with us?" Greg asked.

Big Don assumed assent and told the squatters, "Look, I don't know how the fuck long it'll be before somebody shows up wanting healing, so why don't you come in out of the sun."

They all filed in, and it was very crowded. They

couldn't avoid contact with each other.

"Fuck, dude, you shit your pants? You fucking stink!" Joker told the woman next to him. All of them regretted the move into the booth, and they began filing out.

Then another vehicle pulled up, slowly, indecisively, and then stopped. A man got out and the sign attracted his attention so he read it first before talking.

Big Don approached him. "I dearly hope to fuck you're here for a healing," he said. "You a veteran?" he asked, noticing the man's steel leg.

"No. Farmer," he answered. "Yeah, I think I broke my wrist, it fucking hurts like hell, and I don't have insurance and so fifty bucks is cool, if this guy can do it."

"Take that towel off and let me have a look." The farmer complied. "Fuck, dude, you almost broke your fucking hand off! That looks fucking disgusting! But, you know what, dude, it also looks fucking convincing, so let's see the fifty and then we'll take you over to Big J."

Big Don was jubilant. "Big J, you got a patient! Or whatever!"

The farmer followed Big Don into the booth. Big Don stood tall and announced to the waiting listeners:

"Okay, listen the fuck up, dudes. You are about to witness an actual miraculous healing. I hope. We never tried this on people, only on a rabbit.

"Now, this farmer fucked up his wrist. You can all walk past and look at it. You can see for yourselves how crooked and fucking swollen it is. So form a line and let's do it."

As they passed by, a few gagged and hurried out of the booth. But all agreed that this hand could use a dose of healing.

Once they were again squatted in front of the booth, ready to see the healing, Big Don did more announcing:

"Big J is going to breathe on this man's face, and that should heal him. So Big J, breathe away!"

Everyone waited tensely, inching back and forth for a clearer view. Big J walked up to the farmer, put his face close to the farmer's face, and breathed a long, slow breath on the man. The man turned his head away with a look of disgust at the stream of bad breath.

The squatters all gasped and exclaimed loudly, jumping up and pointing and some rubbing their eyes and others slapping the tops of their heads, all unable to either believe or disbelieve what they had just witnessed.

The wrist was completely normal. The farmer flexed it, opened and closed his hand, and said, "Dude, that's the best fifty bucks I ever spent!"

Then the farmer glanced down and noticed that his steel leg was missing. In its place was a perfectly normal human leg.

"What the fuck did you do to my beautiful steel leg?" the farmer screamed. "I paid twenty fucking thousand bucks for that leg! I love it! What the fuck did you do with it? Where is my fucking steel leg? Turn around, let me look! Where the fuck is it? Change it back! Now!"

Big J said, "Oops."

So the farmer turned to Big Don. "Make him change my leg back, asshole! Now!"

"Oh, like I can do that," Big Don said. "Look, sorry about the leg, okay? Nothing Big J or I can do about that. Consider it a fucking bonus."

The farmer shook his fists in the air, stamped his feet, and screamed, "My friends call me Legman! Fuck! Fuck! Fuck!"

He calmed down after a few moments, and finally said, "At least give me my fifty bucks back."

"Oh fuck you," Big Don said. "Your wrist is healed, isn't it?"

The farmer stared at Big Don, then at his wrist, then at his feet, and then sloughed away, grumbling audibly all the way to his vehicle.

Meanwhile, the campers in the booth were struggling to contain their laughter, waiting for the farmer to leave so they could bust out.

Joker slapped his thighs, choking on his laughter.

"Where's my leg? I love that leg!"

Greg burst out, "Where is it? Where did you put it?"

Big Don shouted, "I want my fifty bucks back!"

The squatters, however, had witnessed their first ever miraculous healing, and they weren't laughing. They murmured but mostly they were severely stunned.

When the campers quieted down enough, Big Don announced:

"Well, that was fucking worth ten bucks, right? So you got your money's worth and I got to shit, so let's close this down for the day and go home."

Somewhat like zombies, the squatters stood up and wandered to their vehicles, not speaking much with each other at all.

Big Don turned around and said, "Let's head back to camp, at least me because I have to take a dump, okay?"

Joker said, "Yeah, I got to take a dump, too."

Keefer said, "Me, too."

Greg said, "And me."

Roland said, "I can try. I already shit once this morning."

Big J said, "Yeah, me, too, I worked up a good

one here."

Later, back at camp, after whiling away the afternoon, it was burrito time under the tree, and time for group discussion, according to Big Don's agenda.

"Well, it was fucking amazing," Joker said. "I mean, the wrist was no fucking surprise, but the leg, that was fucking amazing!"

"Yeah," Big Don noted, "We can call it total body healing now, so no more fucking complaints! What an asshole! Who wouldn't prefer a normal fucking leg?"

Joker laughed and said, "Maybe he can say he never got his steel leg and get his twenty thousand back!"

"Anyway, let's talk about how we go about this," Big Don said. "I think we're ready for the big time. Look, we got a dozen people to come out just from local rumors, right? My gut tells me that tomorrow starts the big time.

"We got a hundred bucks in the kitty," Big Don went on. "Is that enough to rent a big tent? Anybody know?"

No one answered, but Greg was searching. After a moment, he said, "Looks like we could rent something suitable for that, but we have to fucking go get it and set it up. Otherwise, just delivery and set up is more than a hundred.

"Look," he went on. "I think you're right that

tomorrow will be a big day. That means our kitty will get fat, right? So the day after tomorrow, we can afford to have this shit fucking delivered and set up for us. Tomorrow we do the best we can with what we've got, relax, and eat burritos."

That proposal eliminated a day of labor, getting and setting up the tent, so everyone immediately agreed. Greg pushed buttons until he had reserved the tent delivery for two days hence. "Done," he announced.

Roland asked, "Done? What if we don't collect enough tomorrow to pay for it?"

Big Don took over. "If we don't get enough to pay them, we just don't fucking pay them. Fuck them. Simple."

"With the tent," Keefer said, "that'll attract more people, I think, and we'll be collecting every day so I don't think we need to fucking worry about debt here."

"Actually," Big Don said, pensively, "why not find out just how much we can collect? We put subject to change on the sign, right? Let's try a thousand bucks and see what happens."

Roland proposed, "How about this? Anybody willing to pay a thousand bucks is first in line, then the ones who'll pay five hundred are next, then one hundred."

Greg asked, "So what do we do to keep them straight, sell tickets?
Keefer said, "We could rubber stamp their hands

---

like at night clubs."

"Totally cool idea!" Greg agreed. So, who's got some rubber stamps?"

No one spoke. Finally, Keefer said, "Fuck me! Am I the only one who's got anything? Fuck!"

Roland said, "I'll give you a hand."

They went off, then returned. Keefer said, "Okay, I found two rubber stamps. They're self-inking so we don't need a stamp pad."

"Fucking great! So what do they say? What's on them?"

Keefer said, "One says, Fuck You, Asshole, and the other says, Eat Shit and Die. Maybe I could shave off a few words."

Big Don said, "No, leave them just like that! We'll use the Fuck You, Asshole as the thousand buck stamp, and the Eat Shit and Die as the five hundred. The one hundred get shit. That will fucking work great!

"Okay, so that's the plan," Big Don summarized. "We just do our best tomorrow, collect the bucks, get the tent, and sail on into our future success! That about it?"

They all agreed and passed the weed.

The next morning, at 9:45am promptly, a cacophony of car horns was not the only sound the campers heard. There was also a siren.

They quickly gathered under the tree.

"What the fuck is Malone doing here?" Keefer said, staring at the small cloud of dust from the site.

"Maybe somebody gave that dumb fucking cop some gas money!" Joker laughed.

"Well, it's time to go to work, let's go see what that fucker wants," Big Don said.

When they arrived at the site, they saw Malone's police car pulled up close to the booth. When Malone saw them arrive, he got out of the cruiser and limped to the booth.

"Malone!" Big Don greeted.

"Okay, what the fuck are you guys up to here? Fuck, I heard all kinds of stories and it adds up to a scam. I'm going to shut your asses down!"

"Hold on, Malone, just a fucking minute," Big Don said with a calm smile. "This is your lucky day! We're going to heal that fucking leg of yours! If we don't, then you shut us down. And we know that Big J can do legs. He fucking changed a steel leg into a real one. So, ok?"

"You trying to tell me that you got real healing going on here? Who can do that? Somebody who can do that would be famous, right? And I never heard of nobody like that, especially out here."

"Malone, just give it a fucking try, will you? It'll only cost you a thousand bucks to have that leg healed like fucking new."

"Fuck you, a thousand bucks!"

"Well, five hundred then."

"Still fuck you!"

Okay, a hundred bucks or go home. Ok?"

Malone thought about it. "If it doesn't work, I get my hundred bucks back?"

"Absolutely!" Big Don said. "And we haven't given out a refund yet!"

Malone agreed. Big Don said, "Of course, the hundred dollar tier puts you at the end of the line, behind the big money. You don't mind waiting, do you?"

"Fuck you!" Malone said. "I go first to see what this shit is about!"

Big Don relented. "Okay, let's go, let's get this show on the fucking road."

Meanwhile, Keefer had been making the rounds, stamping hands. There were about forty people, all complaining about the increase in prices because they had all heard they could get a healing for fifty bucks. But three did agree to the thousand bucks, only because of the money-back guarantee.

Malone was first. Big J breathed on him and his leg was restored, just like that. Malone coughed on the bad breath.

Malone was completely speechless and staggered for a moment before walking smoothly to his car, ignoring everyone. He left, presumably having changed his mind about shutting them down.

The workday lasted until afternoon, and at the end of it, Dan counted five thousand four hundred dollars.

Most of the healed did not leave. They stayed to talk with the others, comparing conditions that had been healed and marveling together at what a wondrous person Big J was.

A few of them had heard speculation that Big J might really be the second coming. It was easy to argue against, but then, it seemed there must be a possibility.

"He does say he was in Nazareth two thousand years ago," one said.

"But he's not at all like we expected! He's gross!" another said.

"Do you think he's one of those false prophets?"

"I don't know. He's pretty good at what he does."

"Oh, a healer is one thing, the rapture is quite another!"

The healed finally dispersed and the campers returned to camp, ate a few burritos, and generally celebrated. Everything went so well today! Even with a lot of confusion! That Malone bit was just too fucking precious! We can pay for the tent, dudes!

"Tomorrow, the tent arrives, early, so it'll be set up by ten," Greg said.

"So, who's getting up early to supervise this?" Big Don asked.

"Fuck me, I'm tired," Roland said.

"Just let them fucking surprise us!" Joker said. "We can all sleep in!"

"What the hell. How can they screw up setting up a fucking tent?" Big Don said. "Let's sleep in."

When they arrived at the site the next morning, the tent was erected with the sides rolled up for ventilation. It was covered with the thick cloud of dust the traffic had raised.

There were several hundred people gathered in and around the tent, almost entirely women because the men didn't believe in that faith healing shit.

Big Don took a position at the show time end of the booth, and summoning a stentorian voice, announced:

"Listen up! Dickheads, listen up! I've got bad news, so listen up! Yesterday, Big J healed about forty people and that pushed us into overtime. So forty is about the most that Big J can heal in one day. It looks like there are three or four hundred of you, so that means that most of you are fucked for today.

"So, three tiers. Thousand buck people go first. Hands up, how many thousand buck people have we got?"

First, about thirty hands went up, then very quickly, about thirty more.

"Well, fuck, that overloads us right there. Thousand buck people, form a line over here. The rest of you come back tomorrow."

There were shouts of disappointment and anger. Joker jumped up with his great idea.

"Balloons! The fucking balloon idea! Listen, dudes," addressing the crowd, "we'll get balloons and Big J will blow them up and you let the balloon blow on your face and you're healed! We can do hundreds a day that way!"

The grumbling quieted some. "When do we get these balloons?" one demanded.

"Tomorrow!" Joker shouted. "We'll have them tomorrow!"

"But you can pay and get stamped today if you're a thousand buck-aroo!" Big Don said. "That'll save your place for tomorrow."

Keefer went down the line with the rubber stamp as quickly as he could, and he soon had sixty-two thousand dollars in his pocket.

"Mine says, Fuck You, Asshole!" one man complained.

There were still dozens of people waiting or milling around when the two o'clock closing time came around. Big Don checked with the other campers, and they decided to continue until everyone was healed. It went on until after four o'clock.

They returned to the camp exhausted. But rich. After making their bathroom runs, they slouched into their seats near the tree, Keefer wiping his forehead with a bandanna, Roland closing his eyes and resting his head back, Greg quietly staring off into space, and Big Don settling into his getting ready to speak position. Joker was smiling as usual and looking at his hands. Big J was tired, too, and slumped, holding his chin in his hands

After several minutes of breath catching, Big Don began.

"So, balloons, huh? Maybe that'll work, who fucking knows, but where do we get hundreds of balloons by tomorrow?"

Greg asked, "So, anybody got balloons? Or condoms, maybe?"

They shrugged their shoulders and looked at each other.

"Fuck me!" Keefer said. "I probably have some fucking balloons, not many."

Roland said to Keefer, "I'll give you a hand."

"Keefer, that trailer of yours," Greg began, "I don't know, dude, but it's like Aladdin's lamp. Does this shit just appear in there because you look for it? Or do you really have some of every fucking thing?"

"Well, one balloon is enough to test with, anyway, because we still don't fucking know if this shit will work," Big Don said.

"No, you're going to fucking shoot the rabbit again? Really?" Roland said.

"Well, what the fuck?" Big Don answered. "So it feels like fucking burrito time to me," he continued, "and then we'll do the test. Sound cool?"

When they had finished their burritos and beers, they discussed the test.

Keefer and Roland had found only two balloons. They decided to use one for the test, and save the other one.

Next, Big J blew up the balloon, pinched it closed, and handed it to Keefer. Who handed it to Greg. Who handed it to Roland. Who handed it to Joker, saying, "You hold it, this is your fucking idea."

Joker took the balloon, taking over the pinch. "What do I do, tie it closed?" he asked the campers.

"No, because then how can we untie it?" Greg said. "We need a pincher thing that unpinches, I don't know what, but something that lets us open the balloon without popping it. So any ideas?"

After a moment, Keefer had an idea. "We could cork the balloon. Then it would be pinch, pull out, and release, smooth.

"If we had some ham," Big Don said, "we could have ham and eggs, if we had some eggs! Now it's fucking corks! Well, maybe we ought to fucking try that. Anybody got a cork?"

It seemed that no one had a cork, except Keefer.

"Oh, fuck! Me again?" he said.

I'll give you a hand," Roland said. They want off to Keefer's trailer, hunted for a while, then returned with a cork from a wine bottle.

"Good work!" Big Don said. "Now, somebody blow up a fucking balloon and stick this cork up its ass!"

Roland did it, blew up the balloon and pulled the opening of the balloon over the cork as he also pinched the neck of the balloon. "This is really fucking awkward," he said. But he finally got it and he set the balloon on the ground in the middle of their circle, and they all watched it.

"It fucking works!" Joker said. "Look at that fucker, it's not leaking!"
But after another moment, it was clear that the air pressure was slowly pushing the cork out. They

---

watched. The cork didn't pop out; it just puffed out, leaving a flaccid balloon.

"Well, fuck that!" Keefer said. "Who's got the next idea?"

"Sonofabitch!" Big Don said. "That could have fucking worked!"

"How about this? We roll up the neck of the balloon and hold it with a paper clip?" Greg suggested.

"Fucking great, now it's paper clips," Big Don said.

"I do not have fucking paper clips," Keefer said. "I don't do officy shit."

Big J finally spoke up. "Look, dudes, it is a whole fucking lot easier me to blow on a face than it is to blow up a balloon, and I'm not going to blow up hundreds of fucking balloons. Fuck, just line people up and parade them past me as fast as I can breathe. Fuck the balloons."

"Good news, Frisky," Roland addressed the rabbit, "You're not getting killed again today!"

"Okay, we'll go with the tight lineup idea," Big Don said. "Next, let's talk about money, because we've got almost a million bucks in our kitty. We could do something."

Greg put his phone back into his shirt pocket. He'd been searching for somebody to deliver balloons like immediately.

"Let's ask Big J," Greg said, and turning to Big J, "what do you think, Big J? You want to grow the business?"

"Fuck, no!" Big J said. "I am beat to shit from today, so that's all I can fucking handle."

"Huh, well, fuck then," Big Don said. "So we just divvy the money up between us?"

"And sit out here in the middle of fucking nowhere with bags of money?" Greg asked. "We'd better spend it as fast as possible, starting with some fucking security!"

"Whoo! We can start our own fucking city, dudes!" Joker said.

"Yeah, and maybe our own fucking army," Don said sarcastically. "Look, we got a problem here. What the fuck are we going to do? Suddenly, we can fucking afford anything!"

"Until the robbers come and take it all the fuck away," Greg said.

"Yeah, yeah, get fucking boring," Big Don said. "Here I am, thinking about cathedrals, but I know you're right, we need some fucking security here first."

"We need a fucking fence for one thing," Keefer said.

"With a gate for the cars to enter," Roland said. "We can close the gate after four hundred cars."

Greg pointed out, "That'll just make them come piled six in a car. Better to stamp the four hundred at the fucking gate and then close it."

"And pave a fucking parking lot!" Keefer said. "That dust storm could travel over here."

"And build a stage with a safe room!" Joker said. "I saw that shit on TV!"

"Like we could do that tonight, asshole!" Big Don said. "But hey, it's not a bad idea, just we got to do some security right away."

"How many guns we got?" Greg asked.

"Fuck, guns?" Roland said.

"Whoo! Blow the motherfucking heads off those fucking bad guys!" Joker said, firing shots in the air with his finger.

Big J had fallen asleep with his forehead resting on his knees. Suddenly, he tipped forward on his stool and landed on the ground. The campers laughed as he stood up slowly, brushed himself off, then sat back down.

"Okay, what the fuck did I miss here?" he said.

"Looks like we're building a fence and a parking lot and a stage with a safe room. That's so far," Big Don answered.

"Sure, so when is all this happening?"

Big Don turned to Greg. "We've got the bucks,

Greg. How about seeing how much speedy service we can buy?"

"Okay, I better do this in my trailer because I'll need to make a lot of fucking notes."

Greg tackled the fence first. He looked up fencing contractors and began making calls. Most were closed and had recordings, but one did answer.

"We need to fence in about an acre of desert near Quartzsite, and we need it tonight. Can you do it?"

"I'm paying cash and I have buckets of it."

"A temporary fence? You can do that by morning?"

He moved on to the stage and safe room.

"I need a stage with a safe room, and I need it tomorrow."

"I'm paying cash and I have buckets of it."

"We've got a healer out here and he's pulling in buckets of money every day. Big J, maybe you heard about him."

"Yeah, him. So we got the bucks."

"Dude, we had fucking fights break out today! We need security! Kind of funny, though, watching a bunch of old cripples trying to fight."

"Fuck the building permit! It's BLM land so who

gives a fuck?"

"Big enough for six people."

"Really? A prefabricated safe room? How quick?"

"Well, how long does it take to get one from Houston?"

"Fuck that. How long by helicopter?"

"What I'm saying is, you get in a helicopter now and go get that safe room and bring it here tomorrow."

"An extra hundred thousand bucks."

And within forty-eight hours, the power of money created a decent stage with steps on both sides and a safe room at the back. The acre was fully fenced in, with an asphalt parking lot for two hundred fifty vehicles.

By 10:30, four hundred thousand-buckers were gathered in the fenced area, hands properly stamped with Fuck You, Asshole.

Roland wandered among the crowd, listening to their conversations. Two older women were talking, heads close together.

One said, "Do you suppose he really is the second coming?" The other said, "Lord, I hope not, not yet! I still have two years left on my term policy!"

All of the campers had checked out the safe room. They each had a key on a chain around their neck.

It was nicer inside than any of their RVs, except maybe for Greg's. There was a beer cooler and it was full. There was a DVD player and a small library of books and discs. Six handguns were mounted on one wall. Was it worth three hundred thousand dollars? None of them cared.

"Okay, folks," Big Don announced. "Let's get started! Make a line and put your hands on the shoulders of the person in front of you. When you reach Big J, turn your head to look at him and let him breathe on you. Then move on. If you don't have legs or some shit like that, just ask somebody for help. You're first," he said, pointing to an old so man bent over that the woman behind him had her hands on his back.

The day proceeded rather smoothly. Getting people to leave after their healing was a problem, but Roland, Joker and Keefer formed a brigade to escort them directly to their cars.

Financially, at the end of the day the kitty was well into the black. They locked all of their cash in the safe room, locked the gate, and headed for camp for some burritos.

Chapter 5

BLM Ranger Rosie got a report that she had another hippie enclave to get rid of. The report didn't tell her that there was something more going on than just hippies camping on BLM land.

It was the seventh day of doing business with the fence and stage. Each day went smoother than before, and the campers were feeling exultant.

Then there was an incident. Big J was visibly exhausted and around noon his hands began to bleed. And his ankles. It wasn't a lot of blood, but it was red and several people noticed it immediately.

"Look! Look! His hands! He really is the second coming!"

People gasped. One heavy woman gasped so strongly that it made her fart.

Big Don sprang into action. "Come on, let's get him the fuck into the safe room!" They all gathered in the safe room, unsure of what might develop outside.

They turned to Big J, looking at his hands and haggard face.

Big J said, "Fuck, I am fucking weary. Out of breath. And now this bleeding shit."

Greg asked, "Big J, you think you can heal yourself?"

"Maybe. Give me a bag."

Joker said, "Paper or plastic?"

"I don't see any bags in here. What's it for, Big J?" Roland asked.

"I'll blow in it and then push that breath on my face. Might work."

Keefer said, "Well fuck, dude, I've still got a balloon in my pocket!" and handed it to Big J.

Big J inflated the balloon, and then released the air on his face. He was immediately rejuvenated. Hands and ankles were healed, his face was young and refreshed.

Big Don said, "Well, fuck, dude! If I'd known you could do that, I'd have left the fucking gate open!"

"You better let me hang on to that balloon," Keefer told Big J.

"So are you back in business now, Big J?" Big Don asked. "I'll go quell the fucking crowd."

The people were all talking loudly, trying to hear each other. Big Don took center stage, put his palms out and shouted, "Shut the fuck up, motherfuckers! Listen the fuck up! Big J needed a breather because he ran out of breath. He's rested now and he's coming back out in a minute. So straighten out that line and shut up!"

"What about the stigmata?" a senior woman demanded?

"What the fuck is stigmata?" Big Don challenged. "Speak English!"

"The blood! His hands and his feet! I saw the blood! He's the second coming!"

"Big J is no fucking second coming, believe me. He's just a healer, so forget about that second coming shit!" Big Don fabricated.

"The blood!"

"There is no motherfucking blood! You're seeing things! Just a minute." Big Don knocked on the safe room door and brought out Big J.

They went to center stage. Big Don said, "Big J, show her your hands!" The woman stared at Big J's palms, looking for any evidence of a wound, but she saw nothing and slowly got back in line.

There were no more incidents for the next several days, but one afternoon, Ranger Rosie pulled up to the gate and sounded her siren.

"Oh, fuck! It's BLM!" Roland said.

"It's a woman! Let's blow her motherfucking head off!" Joker said.

Big Don said, "Will you shut the fuck up? I'll go talk to her."

Ranger Rosie was standing at the locked gate, and Big Don spoke through the gate. "Can I help you?"

"What the hell have you got going on here? I expected a few campers, but this is a damned carnival! Anyway, it's got to go, immediately. You're on BLM land."

"Have you heard about Big J, the healer? That's what we're doing here, healing people. How about you, you got anything wrong, any physical complaints? Big J can fix you right up!"

"Huh!"

"Just look at the people leaving here, they've all been healed. And look and those still in line, all crippled and staggering. See for yourself! We are healing people here!"

"Huh! Well, what the hell, I'll give it a try. I do have a bad shoulder. Cyst on my neck."

"Maybe you could give us thirty days notice?"

"We'll see. Let's get this over with."

Big Don led her on stage, interrupted the line to let Ranger Rosie catch a breath, and then they stepped aside.

"Feel any different?" Big Don asked her.

"Well, damn, yeah! Impressive! Too bad I have to put you out of business."

"Thirty days notice?"

"You can expect the demolition crew next couple of days. If that sideshow is still standing, they'll blow it up."

"What, fucking dynamite?"

"Saves a lot of demo time, and out here, why not? And they'll tear down the fence, and then this will be clear land again."

"You bitch! You can't give us a motherfucking break?"

"I just gave you a break. Two days. First I said immediately, now you got two days."

"You got healed for free and you're still a fucking bitch? Fuck you! Get your fucking ass out of here before I kick it to South Boston!" Big Don's gallant courtesy had vanished.

Ranger Rosie looked up at Big Don, a bit intimidated but she managed to say, "Two days. Thanks for the healing."

Big Don decided to save the discussion until

burrito time. He returned to the stage and helped to shepherd people.

"So what did she say?" Greg asked.

"In two days, they dynamite this stage."

"Whoo! Fucking dynamite!" Joker said. "What a fucking show that will be!"

"Yeah, well, we'll work out a plan back at camp. Give us some time to think about it," Big Don said. "Meanwhile, let's keep these bucks coming in because it looks like we're fucking going to need them!"

Later, back at camp, eating burritos, they agreed that they needed a new stage location, and may as well move their camp, too.

"Don't go buying any property," Big Don said to Greg. "Lease it, keep us off the property rolls."

"Something remote but not too far from Quartzsite," Roland suggested.

Keefer said, "Well, we can move our shit to another location okay, but moving the fucking safe room is a problem."

"Okay, so we need to lease a couple of acres and move the safe room to the new location. And build a new stage. Agreed?"

Greg went to his trailer to make the calls.

"Yeah, we need the helicopter again. BLM is

blowing us up in two days."

"Fuck yeah, with real dynamite! We got a bitch ranger."

"No shit? The safe room can't be hurt by dynamite? You're fucking with me!"

"My money's worth, got it."

"Listen, please be ready to do the whole show all over again in two days. Just so we get the safe room out of there before BLM figures out how to do it. I'll get the new location to you."

With that settled, Greg moved on to the land lease. He leased two acres for ten years, utilities included, a half-mile outside of Quartzsite. A road led to it.

Greg reported to the campers. "He says the safe room is impervious to dynamite."

Joker jumped up. "Fuck, let's be inside it for the explosion! What a fucking trip!"

"Is that bullshit?" Big Don asked Greg, ignoring Joker.

"Nope. I watched a video of a safe room like ours, watched it dynamited from four sides, and all it did is jump up a fucking foot or so."

"Motherfuck! Well, who wants to be in it? Yeah, I know you do, Joker." They all agreed that it would be fun.

"In the meantime, let's get our fucking RVs moved to the new site. Roland, I think it's time we buy a fucking RV for Big J, right?"

Greg ordered an elegant forty-foot motorhome with three slide outs. They could all do their laundry in it and end their visits to the Quartzsite laundromat.

Forty-eight hours later, Ranger Rosie arrived at the site with her caravan of BLM trucks. The campers arrived early to watch the action.

A BLM backhoe tore the fence down and BLM workers rolled it up into big rolls. The BLM backhoe loaded the rolls onto BLM flatbed trucks. They finished this BLM job before BLM Rosie directed them to the stage.

BLM workers approached the stage, carrying a box and some bags. They returned to their BLM truck for more stuff and the campers took this opportunity to sneak into the safe room.

Safely inside, the campers waited.

Greg said, "If this thing is going to jump up, we'd better protect our fucking heads."

They all agreed that this was a good idea, and they held their seat cushions on their heads. Which left them sitting on bare steel.

"Who's going to take pictures? We need some fucking pictures of this!" Joker said.

"Are we going to get hurt here?" Keefer asked.

"Big J can fix us up if we do, right Big J?" Big Don answered.

"What if Big J gets hurt?" Roland asked.

"We've got the balloon. Big J, blow up the balloon and let me hold on to it. If you get fucking wasted, I'll blow the balloon on you," Keefer said.

Keefer held the balloon pinched closed with one hand, and held his seat cushion on his head with the other.

And just then, Kaboom! and Joker shouted, "Whoo! We're float...!"

Their heads did hit the ceiling and the seat cushions did protect them, but their asses landed on hard steel and they all screamed, "Fuck!!"

Big Don screamed at Joker, "You and your fucked up ideas! Fucking asshole!"

Keefer handed the balloon to Big J, saying, "Do the deed, dude!" Big J released it onto his face, then twisted his head aside and said, "Fuck! My breath smells that bad? Dude!"

Then he made the rounds in the safe room, curing ass.

They opened the door, and stepped carefully through the pile of fragmented stage. BLM had pushed the crowd well back before the explosion.

Ranger Rosie walked up to the campers, seeing the safe room for the first time. "What the hell is that thing? You was in there?" she asked, a bit astonished. "Whoa, what was that like?"

"Not really as great as we expected," Joker said. "We had sore asses for a while there!"

"Well, how do I move that damned thing out of here? Shit!"

"We are happy to help," Greg said, and called in the helicopter to move the safe room.

Soon, the safe house was moved and the campers took a last look at the healing site. They headed for their new and legal camp.

The safe room was already in place behind the stage when they arrived. Workers were still busy on the new stage building, and on the utility lines for the RV hookups. The fence and gate were up. It was burrito time.

In a few more days, they were ready to reopen for healings. Keefer and Joker went into town and put up a sign.

Naked Man's booth seemed to be first choice for gathering, probably because he always had weed and was generous with it. Keefer and Joker walked over to them.

"Hey, Naked Man! Got milk?" Keefer called out.

"Got milk? What the fuck is that?" Joker said.

"Okay, you go, smartass."

"Hey, Naked Man! Got ass?" Joker called out.

"Fucking twerp, that was mine last time!"

"I reconsidered it and found it good," Joker said. "That's a compliment, dude! Besides," he added, "I couldn't think of a fucking thing else."

Naked Man greeted them by holding out a joint. "It's the anarchists!" he said. "How things going out there?"

"We got a new gig out there, dude!" Joker said. "BLM blew us the fuck up with dynamite, so we got a piece of land and we've been setting up shop again."

Martin said, "You know, some old bags, three of them, came by here saying they saw Big J's hands bleed. Couldn't see his feet because of people. That really happen?"

Joker said "Yeah" and Keefer said "No."

Well, which is it?" Martin asked.

"It's what the sane person said, namely me," Keefer said. "That shit, I heard some about that, it never happened. She stood in the heat too long or something. We showed her Big J's hands up close and there wasn't a fucking scratch on them."

"Yeah," Carlos piped up. "They said he probably healed himself, you know, being a healer and all."

Keefer shot a stern look at Joker who wanted to speak. "That would be a good fucking trick!

Physician, heal thyself! For fucking sure, dude."

Martin said, "They think he's the second coming because of the bloody hands and the healings. Has Big J said anything about that?"

"Oh, we asked him about that, of course. He doesn't know a fucking thing about any second coming. He just heals. Starting tomorrow, by the way."

"Well, don't be surprised if you catch some shit about it," Martin said, settling back down.

"What shit?"

"I'm just saying, those old bags, there's no talking them out of it, and they're telling their fucking bridge circles that they've seen the second fucking coming."

"Shit. We tried to kill any talk like that. Because even if he is the second coming, there ain't shit he can do about it anyway. Huge fucking disappointment in that respect." Keefer kicked the dirt.

"But he's fucking amazing at healing!" Joker said.

"Fucking rumors anyway."

"So the other rumor, want to hear it?" Martin asked. Keefer nodded slowly. "The husbands of these old bags are saying that Big J is a false prophet and maybe they're planning something."

"Fuck me! We haven't even fucking reopened

yet!"

When they returned--a much smoother ATV ride on the dirt road—Joker excitedly ran to the others under the tree and shouted, "We're getting fucking raided!"

After Keefer explained, Big Don said, "Fuck, we need a fucking army now?"

"Maybe it's just rumors," Roland said.

"Maybe, but remember, rumors are what got us started," Greg said.

Big Don ordered Joker to report. "And give it to us fucking straight, no bullshit, and no fucking space ships!"

Joker glanced over at Keefer and saw he was still making an adjustment on his ATV, so he reported.

"So all we know is that the husbands are pissed off and maybe they're planning something," Big Don summarized. "Not exactly great fucking spy work!"

"Great fucking reporting, though!" Joker bragged.

"Spy work might be just what we fucking need," Greg said.

"I can just go down the line and ask the women what their husbands are planning," Roland said. "Or ask them after they're healed, that would be better."

Big Don said, "Okay, I think that sounds good enough for now, right?"

Keefer took over. "Why are we still eating fucking burritos?"

Big Don said, "Um, because we have a fucking freezer half-full of them?

"What I fucking mean is, I could be eating steak tips and roasted potatoes here, delivered hot and on time. Fuck the burritos."

"Cheeseburger, fries and a shake!" Joker said, jumping up.

"Well, fuck, why not?" Big Don said. "I wouldn't mind some macaroni and cheese, and maybe a hot fudge sundae."

"Kung Pao Tofu," Roland said.

Greg said, "I'll see if I can get a Japanese bento for myself. Big J, what about you?"

Big J had been learning some Bible stories. He smiled and said, "Bread and wine, of course! Not. A fucking fish, I guess."

"Okay, so that's our menu for tomorrow. I hired an assistant, by the way. She can really deal with this shit! In her own name, too. But right now, I need another fucking burrito," Greg said.

At six o'clock the next evening, they were seated at individual tables and drooling over the array of food before them.

They were always tired at the end of the workday, but this happy meal restored their spirits. Just in time to discuss the impending invasion of the husbands.

"Well, the worst thing I picked up is that they want to crucify Big J as a false prophet," Roland said. "But only two women said that."

"Fuck, two is fucking enough!" Greg said.

"Let's blow their motherfucking heads off and bury them in the desert!" Joker said.

"The two women, or the mob of husbands?" Keefer asked.

"I suppose we should prepare for the worst," Greg said.

"Yeah, but what does that look like?" Big Don asked. "Do we hire some mercenaries?"

"Whoo! Fucking A!" Joker exclaimed.

"I think our business would fall off if we massacre hundreds of husbands," Keefer said.

"The easiest thing would be to just fucking let it happen," Big J said, startling the others.

"Just let you be crucified?" Roland asked.

"Fuck yeah," Big J said. "You know I can heal myself."

"This feels a little like blowing Frisky's

—

motherfucking head off," Roland said.

They all sat quietly considering this plan, or this no plan.

"Isn't it the best way?" Big J asked, breaking the silence.

Slowly, they nodded their heads, looking at each other.

"Well, fuck anyway!" Keefer paused. "Okay, I'll guard the balloon, Big J."

"Next item is tomorrow's menu," Greg said quietly.

They were all full from the catered meals they had just finished. And the thought of watching and allowing Big J's crucifixion took away their appetites.

"Right, same thing again," Greg said.

Chapter 6

The Quartzsite bar was filled today. A dozen or so of the men were older husbands, and they were getting drunk and bitching and moaning about Big J.

They had gripes that the younger husbands did not share. After the healings, their wives were hot and they were not. But worse, their wives were hot for Big J.

Clearly he was a false prophet and somehow needed to be got rid of.

The old, drunk husbands huddled together and decided to do something about it.

They considered beating the shit out of him; and tarring and feathering him, but they lacked supplies for this.

Then one man said, "Let's fucking nail him to a crosh! Fucking second coming fake faker!"

"Yeah, less cruficy the sumbitch!" one man barely said.

"I got a four by, four by four fost, post in my garage!"

"We got bats, right? Basheball bats?"

Having settled on their plan, they returned to their homes for late lunch.

When their wives learned what they planned to do, they did their best to dissuade their husbands. When they couldn't, they wanted to go with their husbands to maybe stop them, the drunk fools.

One thing about women who love Jesus is that they are subjugated by their husbands, who uniformly ordered the wives to stay home.

They learned that the food truck would deliver dinner to the campers by six o'clock, and decided to follow it in.

Before six, the husbands had their trucks lined up ready to follow the food truck to the new site. They knew there wouldn't be anybody there except the campers and Big J.

"Six of them, nine of us," they thought. "And they'll open the gate for the food truck."

"We rush in with baseball bats, grab Big J, nail him to the crosh, and hang him up to dry. Oh, and take pictures!"

The food truck drove directly to the rear of the acreage where the RVs were set up, and the old husbands followed on foot from the gate, sneaking up, stumbling drunkenly. By the time they arrived, the tables had been set up and the meals were being served.

"Which one of you ashholes is Big J?" one man demanded.

Big Don said, "We'll tell you after we eat. Let Big J have his last meal. Sit down. We know what you're up to and it's okay with us."

The husbands were unsure how to respond. The campers all looked like fucking hippies, so they couldn't pick out Big J. And having a last meal is a respectable request. So they sat down.

The campers ate and talked jovially, sharing the amusing moments from the day's work, slowly relishing their desserts, passing a joint, having a beer, belching and farting, and appeared generally at ease in face of the impending crucifixion.

Finally, Big Don stood up and told the husbands, "Okay, men, you can do your little crucifixion thing now. Be gentle, right?"

The men stood up uncertainly and unsteadily, using their bats as canes. They shook out their legs, and one muttered, "Well, let's go. So which one is Big J?"

Big J raised his hand.

"Where's the cross?" one asked.

"It's in Pete frucking truck! Nobody carried it?"

So three men made their way to Pete's truck and the other six loitered, keeping an eye on Big J.

When the three men returned, they all directed the project of nailing the board to make a cross, and the one who brought the hammer and nails secured the board, bending a few nails.

They stood back then, admiring their work. One said, "We better nail him on it while it'sh down because we can't do it up in the fucking air."

It was time to brandish their bats, and they turned to Big J. "You going to give us trouble, ashhole?"

Big J didn't answer, but simply walked to the cross and stretched out on it.

"Nail him down!" one said, and the guy with the hammer put a nail through each palm. He turned to the feet and scratched his head. "I don't got no nails long enough for his feet!"

"Well, fuck, then, just tie them to the post!" So he did that, using a suspender from his overalls.

"Okay, let's get this thing upright."

They lifted the cross from the top, but as they lifted, the foot of the cross just slid ahead of them, marking a trail through the dirt. They pushed harder, and one man stumbled and grabbed the beard of his neighbor for support.

"Fucking hell! Grab your own beard, you fash mitter!

"Where the fuck is the hole, anyway?" another asked.

No one spoke.

"Nobody dug the fucking hole?" and they dropped the cross to the ground.

"Um, the shovel ish in Pete truck."

"Fuck this shit! Lesh just let him fucking lay there!"

"Let the coyotes deal with this shit!"

"I need a drink. I'm going to the bar."

"Fuck, me too," a few said, and they all stumbled

away in the dark.

Joker and Keefer hurried over to Big J, checking out his hands first.

"These are fucking finish nails, dude! You could have pulled your hands loose any fucking time!" Joker said.

"Oh, for sure," Big J moaned. "But my hands really should be loose before the healing, so how about you guys yank them off on three. Get that balloon over here, Keefer, and let's fill it up."

Keefer held the balloon for Big J, and Big J blew and blew but the balloon wouldn't inflate. Keefer examined it and found a tear.

"Fuck! I had it in my pocket with my keys!"

"Well, get a bag or something! I'm fucking hurting here!"

"Paper or plastic?" Joker said. But nothing was readily at hand.

"Okay, look," Keefer said. "Two guys on each side, we yank the hands off the nails, and we form a bowl with our hands over Big J's mouth for his breathing thing."

They assembled on both sides of Big J. One person on each side was ready to yank with one hand and held the other hand prepositioned in front of Big J's mouth.

On three, they did it. They swiftly yanked the hands, getting their own hands bloody in the process, and then arranged their hands like a bowl. Two were dripping blood on Big J's face.

"Hey, let me save that fucking blood!" Joker said.

"I can sell that shit!"

Big J stood up, wiping the blood from his face with the back of his hand. "Let's grab a fucking beer," he said, stretching.

"Precisely! Let's go home. We've got another busy fucking day tomorrow," Big Don said.

The End

Other Books by the Author

DMC Dynamic Model of Consciousness, by George Arthur Lareau

The Truth At Last! A Discourse on Generated Reality, by George Arthur Lareau

Mind Blow: Understanding Consciousness, by George Arthur Lareau

Create Reality with Morphic Robots, by George Arthur Lareau

Three Peaks: A Model for Understanding Truth, by George Arthur Lareau

A Chat with the Devil: Short Fiction, by George Arthur Lareau

The Game Is Played on a Delicate Foundation, and even better poems, by George Arthur Lareau

Second Coming on the Johnny Show, a comedy, by George Arthur Lareau

My 44 Wives: A True Story of Multiple Personality, by George Arthur Lareau

www.ingramcontent.com/pod-product-compliance
Lightning Source LLC
Chambersburg PA
CBHW061458040426
42450CB00008B/1411